Toni Frissell

PHOTOGRAPHS: 1933–1967

Toni Frissell

PHOTOGRAPHS: 1933–1967

INTRODUCTION BY George Plimpton

FOREWORD BY Sidney Frissell Stafford

ANDRE DEUTSCH

In Association with the
Library of Congress

FRONTISPIECE:
Weeki Wachee Spring, Florida.
Harper's Bazaar, December 1947;
Sports Illustrated, 1955.

First published in Great Britain in 1994 by
André Deutsch Limited
106 Great Russell Street
London WC1B 3LJ

ISBN 0-233-98903 X

Cataloguing-in-Publication Data available for this title from
the British Library

Printed by Horowitz-Rae

The Toni Frissell Collection at the Library of Congress

The Prints and Photographs Division of the Library of Congress preserves the major archive of Toni Frissell's photographs and manuscripts. The most comprehensive existing record of this remarkable photographer's life and achievement, the archive includes more than 300,000 photographic negatives, color transparencies, contact sheets, and exhibit-quality photographs, dating from about 1935 to 1970. The collection also includes Toni Frissell's personal and business papers and a small library of publications that include her work.

The photographic portion of this archive encompasses the major projects and assignments of Toni Frissell's career. The Library holds the original negatives and manuscripts produced during her work as staff photographer and feature writer for *Vogue*, *Harper's Bazaar*, and, later, *Sports Illustrated* magazines from the 1930s through the 1960s. Also in the collection are the negatives and the contact and enlargement prints of military and relief operations during World War II, which Frissell photographed for the U.S. Armed Services and the American Red Cross.

During the 1950s and 1960s, Toni Frissell was commissioned by several corporations and publications, such as Gulf Oil and *Life*, to produce a number of photo-essays. The Library holds most of the negatives and transparencies generated under these assignments.

Toni Frissell also produced a number of books illustrated with her own photographs. These include two titles for children, her *Robert Louis Stevenson's A Child's Garden of Verses* (1944, reprinted 1962) and *The Happy Island* (a 1946 book about Bermuda written by her friend Sally Lee Woodall), as well as a brief illustrated report on St. Paul's School published by the Concord, New Hampshire, boys' school in 1969. The Library holds the contact prints, negatives, and transparencies for those publications.

Throughout her career, Toni Frissell made numerous portraits of friends and members of her extended social circle, both for magazine assignments and on a freelance basis. The Library's archive contains the negatives for these photographs but relatively few prints, except for images of children.

Aside from the photographs, Toni Frissell's collection of papers at the Library of Congress consists of approximately 30,000 manuscripts and related items pertinent to her career and activities from about 1920 to 1971. These include personal and professional correspondence, journals kept on various trips, passports and press credentials, drafts of memoirs and magazine stories, and daybooks and engagement calendars (all these concentrate on the period between 1945 and 1965).

Due to the enormity of the Frissell archive, only portions of the collection are available so far for unrestricted public use. As part of a project in the early 1980s to process materials relating to Washington, D.C., the Library catalogued thousands of Frissell's fashion photographs taken between 1943 and 1962 for Garfinckel's, a department store (LOTS 12439 and 12440). Also processed at that time were photographs of various subjects in Washington, D.C., between 1946 and 1961. These included prominent individuals in public places, such as Gail Whitney and her mother Mrs. Josiah Marvel at the National Gallery of Art (LOT 12438), informal portraits of Stuart Symington in 1951 (LOT 12434), a ball at the Brazilian Embassy (LOT 12435), and a number of local scenes and views of national monuments between 1946 and 1961 (LOT 12433).

Also processed are examples of the photographer's news coverage of World War II. Subjects range from Oveta Culp Hobby, director of the Women's Army Auxiliary Corps, inspecting WAACs in the Washington, D.C., area (LOT 12437), to British military officers stationed in wartime Washington (LOT 12432), to American National Red Cross chairman Norman Davis (LOT 12436). Examples of her work closer to the front are Frissell's studies of civilian life in bombed London in 1945 (LOT 12457), photographs of the airmen and headquarters of the Eighth Air Force (LOT 12458), portraits of American generals serving in the European theater (LOT 12459), and the 332nd Fighter Pilot Squadron of African-Americans stationed in southern Italy (LOT 12447).

The processed portions of the collection are readily accessible to researchers in the Prints and Photographs Reading Room at the Library of Congress. Currently, access to the unprocessed portion of the archive is granted on an appointment basis to those engaged in advanced scholarly or biographical research. (Written requests should be directed to the Chief, Prints and Photographs Division, Library of Congress, Washington, D.C. 20540.)

Since the Library acquired the Frissell collection in 1971, selections of Toni Frissell's work have appeared in numerous studies of the history of fashion photography. Of particular note are several books marking significant anniversaries of the publications *Vogue* and *Harper's Bazaar*. The photographer herself collaborated with Holland McComb on *The King Ranch, 1939–1944: A Photographic Essay*, based on her earlier photographs and produced in 1975 by the Amon Carter Museum in Fort Worth, Texas, and Morgan and Morgan Publishers.

To foster a wider knowledge of Toni Frissell's work, the photographer's heirs have dedicated to the public all rights they have in her work. Conditions governing work-for-hire may still apply for the publication of certain images.

Beverly W. Brannan
Curator of Photography
Prints and Photographs Division
Library of Congress

Jacqueline Kennedy Onassis made an impossible dream a reality
in this extraordinarily beautiful book. It is only fitting therefore that
Toni Frissell, Photographs: 1933–1967
be dedicated to her.

—SFS

FOREWORD

With dog Hugo
at Stony Brook Harbor.
Vogue, June 1973. Photograph by
Sidney Frissell Stafford.

Toni Frissell was my mother. Being the focus of her camera through two children's books and much of my childhood was an adventure full, for the most part, of fun.

We lived at St. James, Long Island in "Sherrewogue," a big white 1689 house on the water in a cove opening onto the Stony Brook Harbor. It was an ideal place to grow up, and for my mother an ideal setting for her camera.

We had an odd assortment of animals—dogs, peacocks, a donkey, a goat, my horse brought back from a photographic trip to the King Ranch, and a diabolical Shetland pony named Kitt.

We had many inanimate props, too: pony carts, kites, a fleet of canoes, duck boats, sail boats, surf boards, and motor boats. And a pair of merry-go-round horses that were forbidden territory except when they were the focus of my mother's camera. (Though we did manage a few rides on the sly.)

Toni Frissell with son
Varick, husband Mac,
daughter Sidney, and dog
Robespierre on the roof
of the stable at
"Sherrewogue," St. James,
Long Island.
Photograph by
Frances McGloughlin-Gill.

There were children's parties with puppet shows for my brother and myself, and, later, for my two children, productions staged by my mother not only for our joy but to capture that joy through her looking glass to be recorded forever for the enjoyment of others.

Because I was so often the subject, it took me years to recognize the quality of what had been around me hanging on all the walls of Sherrewogue and pasted in the big, red scrapbooks that recorded each year of Toni Frissell's life and work. Eventually I realized that, though diverse in subject, her photos all had the same theme: great beauty and style and an appreciation of the happier moments of life. Even in her World War II work, when she spent time on the front, she recorded the poignant moments—a soldier decorating his helmet with wild flowers, a pilot in a briefing room with a dog on his lap. So many photographers make their names on tragedy, but Toni Frissell's theme was the richness of life.

I have often thought that she sought these moments in order to shut out the sorrow that had streaked her earlier years: the violent deaths of her two older brothers and the death of her mother.

Toni Frissell Bacon and
Sidney Frissell Stafford
photographed by Horst.
Vogue, 1955.

As her daughter I can attest that Toni Frissell was multifaceted. She was incredibly chic. She was completely impractical. She was fearsomely competitive and unbelievably pushy. She was adventuresome and whimsical. She loved men and disliked most women unless they were as nonconforming and had as much flair as herself.

As mother and daughter we loved each other but fought like hell. She admired and praised my photography, but when I assisted her I was forbidden to use my camera. Watching her work taught me a great deal. Perhaps one of the most important lessons was her enthusiasm with her subjects, the way she made everything such fun. She was always playing with new equipment, from Widelux cameras to infrared film. She insisted that she was not a technician, but she experimented constantly; the famous Frissell underwater fashion shots were certainly a first. She loved to be photographed herself, but there too she had to be the director, as I learned when I was shooting the *Vogue* article on her, "I'm 66 and I Love It."

My mother and father's marriage, though unusual, was a good one. They were complete opposites. My father hated large social events involving white tie and tails, while my mother was in her glory at them. My father was his happiest at Sherrewogue in the most tattered clothing, while my mother always dressed in the height of fashion for country living. My father had a mathematical mind, my mother the mind of an artist. They say that opposites attract, and that absence makes the heart grow fonder. This was certainly true in their case, for they were often apart when my mother was on assignment. Their happiest times were in the winters when they went off skiing. Their post-Christmas dinner conversations were totally taken up with where to go for the best possible snow conditions and which ski guide was the best at which place. One of the highlights of my own life was the three months my parents and I spent skiing all over Europe the winter after my graduation from Foxcroft.

Each person has a contribution to make in life. Toni Frissell's contribution was her photography. It is one of the tragedies of the photographic world that her life's work has been buried and forgotten for so long. My hope is that this book, produced in cooperation with the Library of Congress, will reintroduce the art of a truly great photographer. It contains but a small sampling of her work.

—SIDNEY FRISSELL STAFFORD

INTRODUCTION

Toni Frissell
photographing,
her husband Mac and
daughter Sidney in the
foreground.
Photograph by
Frances McGloughlin-Gill.

I t is always surprising, and certainly very pleasing, to discover that a
friend—Toni Frissell—turns out to be a figure of considerable, indeed pivotal
importance in her field. I knew her photographs, of course—they were
published in all the major magazines, but I had not realized that throughout a
career involving not only fashion, but war, sports, and portraiture, she was an
artist of such distinction. However, she has never been accorded her public
due. Her peers—Richard Avedon, Cornell Capa, and Alex Liberman, among
others—all used the word "neglected" to describe Toni Frissell's reputation.

In a sense this collection hopes to rectify this oversight. It is being
published almost six years after her death in 1988 and over twenty years after
she stopped taking photographs. Toni and her husband donated the archive of
her work (over 300,000 images!) to the Library of Congress in 1971. The
sheer enormity of the collection, and the breadth of its scope, have
discouraged the kind of major retrospective accorded certain other

photographers of Toni's generation. It has also caused the Library to be able to make the collection available only on a limited basis. Until now, most have become familiar with Toni's work piecemeal, through the pages of *Vogue*, *Harper's Bazaar*, and other publications. Hence, this book will be the first significant survey of her work. "About time!" has been the reaction of her peers.

I recently talked to a number of them about her work. Different aspects of her style and technique quickly came to mind. One mentioned that she was noted for taking pictures from curious perspectives—describing her lying on her back at the end of a runway to take a picture of a Flying Fortress from under its belly as it took off. She herself tells a charming story in her memoirs about lying on the studio floor, very pregnant at the time, to get a low-angle shot. "I saw next to me a beautifully creased pair of pants and perfectly polished shoes. I looked up and there was Condé Nast himself looking down at me. He said, 'What are you doing down there?' I answered, 'Well, I'm interested in the way it looks from down here.'"

She was praised for her imagination on assignments. She took a series of pictures of a model floating underwater in Weeki Wachee Spring, Florida, dressed in a negligee, its material floating free around her. Two views were expressed about this effect—one which imagined the model as a mermaid, the other as an exceptionally well-turned-out corpse . . . !

On another occasion Toni got permission to get into the orangutan cage at the Bronx Zoo to take pictures of the model from the ape's point of view. The orangutan took the invasion of its premises calmly enough, though at the end of the shoot he picked up a camera case and threw it through the bars at the model.

Toni always saw in her mind's eye what she wanted before she clicked the shutter. She once photographed the Great Hall of the Metropolitan Club in New York the way she thought it ought to look, although this meant six furniture movers had to be hired to remove dozens of tables and chairs and a fifteen-hundred-square-foot Persian rug—all this in the middle of the night. "If it were in the way," she once said, "I'd remove the Statue of Liberty."

And then, of course, there was her subject matter. She loved what she called "a vanishing way of life"—an expensive indulgence that according to her daughter, Sidney, drove her husband, Mac Bacon, into fits of dismay. "I wish I had been an Edwardian," Toni once mourned. "When we give a dinner party, the people who serve wear green jackets and white gloves, but my drawing-room curtains are in shreds."

Small wonder then that one of Toni's most memorable picture essays for *Life* was entitled "The Splendid World of Stanford White"—pictures of some of the architect's most impressive structures (the Newport Casino, a French Renaissance palace in Newport named Rosecliff, the aforementioned

Toni Frissell at a carnival in
Lech, Austria, April 1963.

Metropolitan Club, the indoor tennis court built for the Astor estate in
Rhinebeck, New York). Toni persuaded Stanford White's great-grandchildren
to pose in these places, a charming idea—the children dwarfed by the vast
opulence of those bygone times.

And everyone I talked to mentioned Toni's pioneer efforts in the move to
take fashion photography out of the studio and into the outdoors—the
momentous shift in the thirties whose influence is so clearly evident in today's
fashion magazines.

A bit of background. When Toni came on the scene in the early thirties,
one of the most powerful figures in fashion was Carmel Snow, who had left
the editorship of *Vogue* to become *Harper's Bazaar* fashion editor. Almost
immediately she had fired the magazine's top photographer, Baron Adolf de
Meyer. He was typical of the fashion photographers of the day—his work was
invariably done indoors in studios. For a spread on yachting clothes, the
models were taken indoors and posed in a boat on a painted lake. Though
Meyer was himself a pioneer innovator in studio lighting (he once dropped a
lightbulb down a dowager's bodice to get the effect he wanted), Carmel Snow
thought his style was passé. One of her associates, M. T. Agha, mocked it as
follows: "To be alluring a model must clutch her hips; to be glamorous she
must lean over backwards; to be feminine she must be smothered in flowers."

So in 1932 Baron Meyer was let go and Snow brought in Martin Munkacsi,
a Romanian sports photographer and amateur motorcycle racer who could
barely speak English, as well as Alexey Brodovich, an ex-cavalry officer in the
armies of the czar. The two had a profound effect on the fashion magazines of
the day—Brodovich for his imaginative layouts, and Munkacsi for his
photographs. Munkacsi shot fashion as if it were a news or sports event—his
pictures were more like snapshots than fashion pictures. Indeed he once said,
"All great photographs today are snapshots." Often his seemed vaguely out of

focus, as if taken by an amateur; his most famous fashion shot—because it was the precursor of what was to come—was a slightly out-of-focus shot of a girl on a beach running past the camera in a bathing suit, a cape billowing out behind her, and laughing, as if she were running to greet a friend. Nothing like it had been seen before in a fashion magazine. "Style in motion" was how Munkacsi referred to it. He had an oddly laissez-faire yet practical attitude about his work. "A photograph is not worth a thousand words," he once said. "It's worth a thousand bucks."

It was during this period of innovation that Toni Frissell's work began to appear in fashion magazines. She came in early enough so that through her energy, her choice of subjects, her imaginative eye, she became acknowledged as a pioneer in the development of new photographic techniques. The kind of action shots she took were, by the end of the thirties, replacing formal studio portraiture in every fashion magazine in the country, though her focus on outdoor photography was as much necessity as design. "I don't know how to photograph in a studio," she once admitted. "I never did know about technical points and still don't."

This does not suggest anything slapdash about Toni's approach to the craft. She had various guidelines: "For a long time I liked black and white film because one can more easily catch the instant that never returns. As for color, I prefer the pictures of photographers who understate their color—the off-beat type of picture taken in the fog or in the dust where a small figure is the only bright spot of color or in the rain. Technically, one should take what Kodak says can't possibly be taken. It may be the best picture."

"For me," she wrote, "it is important to capture the flavor of the event. Someone who has gone cubbing and fox-hunting will know the early morning mist that rises in autumn. Another sportsman will remember the sting of sleet as he is caught in a sudden snowstorm on a Rocky Mountain pack trail. I try hard to capture atmosphere in the hope the viewer can smell the flowers on a hillside or feel the joy of a windless Alpine day when the only sound is the hiss of skis running through light, untouched powder."

She felt that sports photography of this sort—which was a substantial part of her career—was a top sport in itself. "To try to catch someone unaware and get a picture of his or her expression when they have shot a bird or won a cup at a field trial is most rewarding. It is a sport to stalk people."

I remember Toni well—an energetic, angular woman, long-necked, with legs that seemed to take her in a number of directions at the same time; her daughter once described the way she got around as being a giraffe's. I knew her when, tired of fashion photography, she started working for *Sports Illustrated* in its early days in the fifties. She had a profound influence on the managing editor; she persuaded him to photograph the sporting world in which she was comfortable, namely the milieu of the affluent: yachting,

RIGHT:
On a fashion shoot.

fox-hunting, polo, the steeplechases, golf, skiing. Toni was not one to be found in the photographers' pens at the ballparks or crouched at court's end at basketball games.

I went with her on one of her "stalking" assignments—to photograph President Eisenhower playing golf at the Newport Country Club. I was to supply a short text to go along with her pictures. Potentially the most dramatic moment of that particular shoot occurred when John F. Kennedy, then the junior senator from Massachusetts, came down the driveway of Hammersmith Farm, his in-laws' "cottage" adjacent to the golf course, to watch the President stroll down the fairway. How Toni knew this was going to happen, I have no idea. But there she was in the street waiting for him, her hope to snap what would have been a remarkable picture—the handsome young senator peering through the bushes at the incumbent President out on the fairway whose office (everyone knew this) Kennedy was planning to run for—a photograph that if successful would have called for what is known in the trade as a double-track . . . a picture that would run across two pages of *Sports Illustrated*.

Standing in the street with my notebook, I watched Toni careering about, her cameras (she often carried three or four at the same time) clanking against each other as she hurried to position herself so that the senator would be in the foreground with the President striding by out on the golf course. The senator didn't seem to mind the frenetic activity going on behind him.

Alas, it didn't work out. The timing was off. *Sports Illustrated* published a photograph of Kennedy in the bushes and a little inset of Eisenhower on the golf course. Since the principals were not in the same shot, Kennedy could just as well have been in the bushes looking at a bird's nest.

Toni and I remained friends for many years. In the early seventies—though I didn't know it at the time—she began to have trouble with her memory. It was a problem that these days would have been diagnosed as the first symptoms of Alzheimer's Disease. In an effort to forestall the encroachment of memory loss, Toni set out to exercise her brain by writing a memoir. She worked on it for three years, and with such intensity that her husband, Mac Bacon, felt that it was the mental effort involved that was causing her memory problems.

The memoir is almost a thousand typescript pages long. It is not a professional writer's work by any means, but rather a vigorous headlong rush—quite slapdash, often insightful and charming—through her remarkably energetic life. In the latter stages of its composition, Toni could not remember what had gone on minutes before, but she could recall the past in vivid detail—not only conversations with acquaintances word-for-word, but invariably what she and others were wearing at the time. Clothes were a passion and continued to be so throughout her life—she was perennially on the Best-Dressed lists. As for the acquaintances, they were invariably the high-born, the notable. She knew or got to know just about anyone worth knowing. Indeed, to the point of brazenness was her uncanny ability to bump into people of distinction who in turn could possibly do her favors:

"I found myself sitting next to the King of Morocco. I couldn't say a word because my mouth was full of terrapin bones." Or, "There, to my surprise, at the airport, was Angie Duke in his coonskin cap." Or, "Rounding Grosvenor Square I bumped into Jock Whitney and Tommy Hitchcock." Or, when the Master of Ceremonies announced "Change Partners!" (at a White Sulphur Springs waltz contest) "to my surprise and his, I found myself confronting the Duke of Windsor." Or, "I sat down next to Mark Hanna on the plane . . . when I developed bronchial pneumonia he moved me into Claridges to recuperate." Or, "my bags were carried by the Polish Ambassador . . . chivalry is not dead." Or, " 'Good morning,' the young Austrian said from his prone position on top of me. 'I was so fascinated watching your skiing gyrations that I forgot to get out of your way. You could have killed us both. My name is Count Felix Schavagotsh.' " Etc., etc.

Born in New York City in 1907, Toni came from a family of adventurers. Her grandparents, railroad people, traveled across the continent to settle in Oregon. Her uncle, who had sailed the seas in clipper ships, was lured to Alaska to search for gold and was eventually lost at sea off its coast in a whaling ship. Her brother Varick (a younger brother, Montgomery, died in a mountain-climbing accident at sixteen) was an explorer and a documentary filmmaker; he was to be a profound influence. Only her father led a more settled life. He was head of St. Luke's Hospital in New York City as well as having many private patients—a Park Avenue doctor.

Toni was named Antoinette, not only after her mother but also a cousin, Antoinette Wood, her godmother, who possessed a considerable fortune. Toni's mother shamelessly subjected her to her cousin's attention at every opportunity, but the two had little liking for the other. The memoir records that on one occasion Antoinette Wood, who must have been insufferable, asked Toni, "Why can't you be beautiful like your other cousins?"—a bit much since these included a girl named Elise Sue, who went on in her college years to become known as "the belle of Princeton"; another, Toni Graves, who in later years was recognized as "the toast of diplomatic Washington"; and Rosamond Pinchot, Max Reinhardt's beautiful ingenue star in *The Miracle*.

Toni was also in disfavor with her cousin's English setter, Peter, who on one visit bit her through the upper lip.

Still she had a childhood which can only be described as privileged—its influence would become obvious in her photographic work. When she was

Switzerland, 1950.

"Mac and I tried another ski run together in deep snow. Each time included a fall; and each time I fell, Mac had to dig me out. I don't know why we went on with skiing, but the life [here] was so wonderful, and we both realized that we would eventually learn to ski." Sidney Frissell Stafford: "And learn they did. My mother and father became great skiers, and each winter one or two months were spent skiing. During the war it was out West, and afterward it was Europe, in all the best ski resorts. It was their passion and their time together. After graduation from Foxcroft I was asked whether I would rather have a coming-out party or three months of skiing all over Europe. I opted for the skiing. It was perhaps the best three months of my life, but also the most fun time I ever had with my mother. I also got the coming-out party!"

Medway Plantation, November 1961. Toni Frissell is across the men's laps. Seated, left to right: Philip Reed, Mac Bacon, Robert Montgomery. Standing: Mrs. Philip Reed, Mrs. Buffy Montgomery, Gertrude Legendre.

taken to the opera she always seemed to be sitting in the Royal Tier, "where a maid would unlock the door and we would hang our coats in a private coatroom where there was a couch—on which Father slept when he got bored." At the Hippodrome she remembers Nervo in a gold costume diving atop a white horse from a lofty platform into a pool below. She recalls Maude Adams in *Peter Pan* and standing on her seat to shout "I do!" when asked if she believed in fairies so that Tinkerbelle's life could be saved. The seats were always the best. "We must have had rich friends," she writes. At Christmas she went to the Andrew Carnegie mansion on Fifth Avenue and Ninety-first Street. The children sang carols. An enormous Christmas tree stood ablaze with real candles, so the butler, liveried, stood between it and the children to protect them. When it was time to give out the presents, he would bend down and carefully retrieve them for Mrs. Carnegie to pass on to the guests.

Naturally there are descriptions of early teenage despairs—arriving at the Boococks for a party carefully outfitted in a white satin dress her mother had bought at Liberty of London ("smocked with blue silk threads, edged with embroidered blue flowers") and having the young Boococks and their friends coming down the stairs wearing paper hats and shouting at the sight of her, "Silky! Silky! Silky!"

Nonetheless, her childhood and adolescence seem idyllic. Many summers were spent in Newport, Rhode Island, at Beacon Hill, a gray-rock castle perched on a hill with a panoramic view of all of Newport. Its owner was Arthur Curtis James, a friend of Toni's father and his patient, an Anglophile who emulated King George V even to his pointed beard. His yacht, *Aloha*, one of the great sights of Newport, had a crew of thirty. His wife was a "magnificent woman with piled-up grey hair turned premature, I suspect, by

Mr. James . . . rather bushy eyebrows that accentuated her sapphire-blue eyes."

Mrs. James's particular fancy in those opulent times was to give pageants—extraordinary productions in which, extravagantly outfitted, she invariably cast herself as a queen, or an empress, or a czarina. The pageants were held at night with an elaborate lighting system hidden among the flower beds to illuminate the proceedings. Orchestras played. On one such occasion Toni recalls Mrs. James appearing with an elaborate decoration on her head— a miniature *Aloha* under full sail on the waves of her hair.

Summer days were spent at Bailey's Beach, "where the ladies bobbed up and down in their black hats." Tennis at the Casino. She remembered Bill Tilden because he was tall and a "bad sport" and Tamio Abe and Yoshiro Ohta because they were "double-jointed and Japanese." Always, she was fascinated by the accoutrements of the very rich. "Mrs. Ogden Goelet's car was a dark maroon open Landau. Around the middle of the car was a hair-thin red stripe with a monogram over the door. In the front sat the uniformed chauffeur with leather puttees, rain or shine. In the back was a folding shell-shaped black leather top that only half-concealed Mrs. Goelet; her large velvet hat topped her dark piled-up hair. On her lap sat a small Pekinese."

Toni's life during her coming-out year was typically frivolous . . . evenings in the nightclubs of the era—Jack and Charlie's, Jimmy Durante's Dover Club, a gangster-run place called the Hotsy Totsy. She writes of the speakeasies looking like parlor cars resurrected with banquettes. At one famous nightclub, Texas Guinan's, where she had gone with her cousin Rosamond Pinchot, the star of *The Miracle*, the red-haired Texan stopped the show and shouted, "Let's give the little girl a hand!"

Largely because of Rosamond, Toni's first serious enthusiasm was with the theater. She appeared twice in Max Reinhardt productions—a role as part of a tree in a German-speaking *Midsummer Night's Dream*, and then in a play entitled *Danton's Death*, appearing in a mob scene in which she was required to yell "phooey!" at the top of her lungs. Alas, she quickly realized she was not cut out for the theater . . . that she would inevitably be relegated to such roles if she continued since few parts existed for actresses as tall as she was.

About that time she began taking pictures, largely because of her older brother Varick, whom she idolized. Also very tall (six eight), popular among their friends, in the Frissell tradition he was very much the adventurer. Though he had a fine baritone voice and for a while considered a career in opera, his interests shifted on an expedition in the Arctic which influenced him to do a documentary on the seal fisheries. He took Toni in hand and taught her the rudiments of photography:

1. Always change film in the shade
2. If you change film in a closet, make sure there's someone on the other side to let you out
3. Mostly, take lots of film. Shoot! Shoot! Shoot!

At first, photography for Toni was a hobby rather than a vocation. At a haut monde dinner in Paris one summer soon after, she replied when asked what sports interested her: *"Je joue le Kodak."*

Nonetheless, far more than photography, life in her early twenties was attuned to the pursuit of happiness, much of it in Europe. She traveled everywhere. At fancy lunches and garden parties she ran, or bumped, into the famous—Margot Asquith, Diana Duff Cooper, Lady Mendl, Katharine Hepburn, Lillian Gish—invariably in her memoir describing what they were wearing at the time. Her accounts are exhausting. The memoir abounds with such lines as "By eleven o'clock we were all organized in Count Berchin's big grey Mercedes."

She fell in love with a deep-voiced, very large Austrian named Frederick Ledebukd, whose lederhosen outfit she admired, as well as his muscular legs. She describes their parting in the memoir: "He put me on the Orient Express train. I threw my arms around him and said, 'God bless you, gentle giant, until we meet again.' He reached up—his long fingers brushing away the tears streaming down my cheeks. The train started to move and went into a tunnel and all was black around me."

There were others, less requited—a young Italian who owned a blue two-seater open Fiat racing car. "The more he liked me," she writes, "the less I liked him. Strange, because he was tall, dark-haired, and good-looking. One night after some sort of putdown on my part, he spent half the night on the street dividing the Casino from the hotel, looking up at my window. He had a silly moon-faced expression on his face and looked like a whipped puppy. I know he was there because I peeked through the shutters."

A more memorable flirtation of those giddy times (Toni refers to them rather shamefacedly as her "bad times") was with the Maharajah of Kapurthala—a gentleman described as ruling a principality in the Punjab the size of the state of Rhode Island from a palace which was an exact replica of Versailles. At a party at Les Ambassadeurs off the Champs-Élysées Toni sat on the Maharajah's left. The next day at her hotel she received a bottle of perfume called "Parfum Maharajah Demasq rouge," which the prince apparently had made up as gifts for his friends.

"Nifty," Toni writes in her diary.

Along with the perfume was an invitation to go for dinner and dancing at the Château Madrid the following evening. She accepted.

"I put on my green dress and white gloves. It was a beautiful night. I went

Toni Frissell's War
Department ID, 1945.

downstairs when the Maharajah announced himself. He was sitting in his
Rolls-Royce. I got in and didn't curtsy, naturally, because how could one do so
in a Rolls-Royce. He took my hand and kissed it. He said, 'I am pleased that
you accepted my invitation to go dancing. I noticed at Les Ambassadeurs that
you dance very well and I like to dance very much.' He looked at me intently
and said "You have a very long neck, like a swan's neck. May I kiss it?' I said
to myself, here we go! So I said to him, 'Oh, Monseigneur, no. You are a king
and I expect you to behave like a king and don't ask such things.' The
maharajah said, 'You haven't been reading your history very well, my dear.
What about Henry VIII? Why, kings often kiss pretty girls.' I said, 'All the
same, I wish to remember you as a very attractive man who has given me a
very exciting time in Paris.' He took my hand that he'd been holding and put
it back in my lap."

A far more serious romance was with a minor-league member of Russian
nobility, Count Serge Orloff-Davidoff. At the fall of the czarist regime he had
escaped from the Crimea with his mother and sister after burying the Orloff
jewels in an apple orchard. A graduate of Cambridge, he had come to the
United States and had a job at Westinghouse Electric. Toni writes of him: "He
was tall with auburn hair and looked as if he were suspended from a
puppeteer's string. He had a small moustache on his upper lip and had
humorous eyebrows over slightly slanting Slavic brown eyes. His fingers were

Italy, 1945.

long and sensitive and he spent hours under his car, 'Elizabeth,' a tin-lizzie Ford. Elizabeth was always immaculate."

On a train back from a vacation in Maine, Toni reports that Serge said, "I don't see how I can live without you. I must go to my boss at Westinghouse and see if I can get a raise. Also I must write my mother to see if she will increase my allowance.' 'Serge,' I said. 'I, too, must get a job so we can make ends meet. I will go to grandfather to see if he will increase my allowance.' "

Adhering to this somewhat quaint vow, Toni took a job selling dresses at Stern's department store in New York City. She hadn't been there for more than a few days when by happenstance she found herself looking over the shoulder of a young artist in the advertising department who was drawing a slinky girl wearing a silver fox collar. Toni took issue with its rather mundane caption: "Chic coat—Good Value." She introduced herself to the artist and asked, "Why don't you pep up the title on that sexy girl you're sketching? Why don't you say, 'Men Don't Like Cold Women'?"

When the advertisement, quickly accepted by the ad department, appeared in the Sunday papers, Toni's mother was so pleased with her daughter's stroke of imagination that she showed the copy to the editor-in-chief of *Vogue*, Edna Chase, who was similarly impressed and hired Toni on the spot.

That year, 1931, despite that early triumph, turned out to be pivotal and traumatic. First, Toni lost her beloved brother, Varick. He disappeared at sea in a series of explosions that sank the *Viking*, his expedition's ship, a few miles off Newfoundland while he was on the way to finish his documentary on the sealing industry.

The Frissells never discovered what had happened to him. Rumors by the dozen turned out to be unfounded. A trapper reported that he had seen a large black dog on Chain Island near the scene of the disaster. A search party investigated and spotted only a pair of silver foxes. Toni was tormented by the thought that her brother had escaped the burning ship with a few others onto an ice pan which had broken off and drifted out to sea in a hard offshore wind . . . little by little breaking up under its human cargo until there was nothing left.

It was not the only heart-breaking event of the year. Her plans to marry Serge came to grief because of the young man's mother—"a round woman with a turned-up nose, slanting eyes and curly grey-blue hair. Her hat was perched on the side of her head giving her a rakish look."

Early meetings with both families had gone well, but at one of them Toni had made the mistake of telling the countess what her job was at *Vogue*: "I have a small, unimportant job writing a little article each month on how to dress with taste, what to choose and buy at small cost and how to put the wardrobe together if one is living on a limited budget."

"Very i-n-t-e-r-e-s-t-i-n-g," the countess had said.

In the meantime, Serge, far from getting a raise in his job at Westinghouse, was fired. He parked "Elizabeth" in front of Toni's apartment and went in to see her. "What I have to tell you is very painful. I am going back to Switzerland. Mother is right. I should meet more Russians and possibly marry one. Only Russians can have a successful marriage without money. You and I, after a few struggling years, would hate each other."

Toni did not take this news easily. She writes in her memoir, "I put my hands over my ears and cried 'No, no, no!' I picked up an empty teacup and threw it with all my force at the black bricks of the unlit fireplace. I turned to ice. 'I would like to see your mother,' I said.

"Countess Orloff was sitting in a straight-backed chair almost like a judge's seat. She had on the usual hat, tilted to one side over her grey-blue curls so she looked slightly ridiculous. Her back was to the light. She pointed to a chair facing the sun, which was hard on my eyes. 'Countess Orloff,' I said, referring to Varick's tragedy, 'How can you be so heartless at this time? Haven't you been reading the headlines?' The countess replied, 'In Russia we also have great tragedies—mass tragedies. I have become used to them," she continued coldly. Then her slanting eyes became cobra slits. 'When a tooth is bad, it must come out. You are a bad tooth.' 'Why am I a bad tooth, Madam?' I asked. 'You and my son are not suitable for each other,' she answered. 'It is a pity I had to make my decision now, but there it is. You are not what I have in mind for Serge. Good Day.'

"For long months I thought of revenges. One of my favorites was having the woman kidnapped, her curly head shaved, and leaving her at a tattoo artist's parlor to have engraved on her: 'I AM A BITCH' in bold letters."

Toni went back to work at *Vogue*, but it was fleeting, only long enough to learn the proper etiquette there. The editors were required to wear hats. Margaret Chase, who wore a blue hat to match her blue hair, explained, "No woman is really well-turned-out without a hat . . . our advertisers like to see us in them." For the same reason, editors were advised never to be seen traveling either by bus or subway.

Put to writing captions, it was soon discovered that Toni was woefully poor at spelling. When she was fired, Carmel Snow called her in and sympathized with her. She gave her some important advice: "Toni, take up photography seriously. Your brother had such talent. Let me see what you can do."

That summer (1931) Toni brought a camera with her to Newport. Taking pictures was as much a therapy as anything else—her mother now seriously ill; the memory of her brother; Varick, lost at sea; her romantic life in disarray.

One morning she was sitting with her mother on the balcony outside her room. As the two of them watched the meadow grass swaying in the wind, a contented look on her mother's face, Toni's inner voice began to speak: "Get out your Rolliflex and get to work and experiment. Look at that field of waving grass. Take pictures on location. Why not make nature and my world the picture studio?"

She started by taking pictures of the sky, imagining what her models would look like outlined against it. An irate golfer discovered her lying on her back in a bunker of the Newport Country Club golf course. She was too embarrassed to tell him what she was doing.

Her first model was Eleanor Young, a young girlfriend of a socialite acquaintance, Willy de Rham, "a great lover of pretty girls, who had numerous crushes and had just found himself a new beauty." She took pictures of Eleanor running through the fields with her hair flying. She took others—Josie Cutting, dressed in riding clothes standing with her horse and leaning over a fence . . . Minnie Cushing and Edith Gray crabbing . . . "it was a calm, slightly foggy day and their figures were reflected in the still water."

This early photographic career was one, as Toni puts it, of "starts and halts." Her first picture appeared in *Town and Country*—a portrait study of a friend, Phyllis Burn, sitting at an apartment window at 1 Sutton Place with the Queensborough Bridge in the background. Blowing up such pictures to full-page size, she made the rounds to show them to editors. Bettina Ballard of the editorial staff of *Vogue* said Toni behaved like an Armenian rug salesman pushing his wares. *Vogue* succumbed and offered her a contract.

Working hard at her craft, she got to know the famous photographers of the time and learned from them—among them Edward Steichen, who was then specializing in photographing celebrities for *Vanity Fair* against black and white backgrounds. He invariably did his work indoors in his own studio, which was a converted stable in the sixties between Park and Lexington Avenues. He was intrigued with Toni's use of natural settings and pressed her to continue with that technique. She apprenticed briefly with Cecil Beaton. He also photographed indoors, for many years using a small box model he had started with in childhood. Diana Vreeland, an editor of *Vogue* at the time, said of this camera that the noise of it going off (*Tw-aang*) sounded exactly "like a rhinoceros coughing." Condé Nast was persuaded to buy him a new model. He did his work with it usually at his apartment in the Ambassador Hotel. Toni's job was to find background *objets* for his shoots—a crystal chandelier, a lace window curtain, a pair of flying gold cherubs, a baroque mirror, a fortune-teller's glass ball, a quilted mattress pad, angel-hair Christmas trimmings.

Toni writes of him: "He made every woman he photographed both elegant and beautiful . . . with transparent skin." One of his favorite models was a young woman named Princess Paley. On one occasion, Beaton was photographing her in his room at the Ambassador in a great canopied bed, wearing very little, with Serge Lifar, from the ballet, "about to rape her" in what was supposed to represent a scene from *Le Spectre de la Rose.*

"At that precise moment," Toni writes, "Margaret Case of *Harper's Bazaar* opened the door of the bedroom. 'Oh, my goodness, how chic,' she said, backing out and closing the door."

Whatever Toni learned from the great indoor portraitists of the time, she preferred to photograph outdoors . . . she took her models outside to natural settings even when they were dressed in furs or evening gowns. She wanted them to look natural, the wind in their hair and blowing the clothes away from their bodies. It was an innovation . . . as was the practice of using her young friends as models . . . society belles Patsy Pulitzer and Joan Patterson. These novel approaches were met with approval at *Vogue*. Carmel Snow wrote a staff memorandum about Toni's selection of nonprofessionals as models: "I am told that the reason we use the Pulitzer-Patterson type so little is that the photographers prefer to use the old-time models, who are too skinny for the modern idea of beauty . . . Do believe me when I say that the average reader, looking over both *Vogue* and *Harper's Bazaar* is sick to death of this type of model both magazines are using. There are many beautiful American girls, and I think that photographers should be flexible enough to get their eye in for the new type."

Instrumental in Toni's success was Condé Nast himself, the stiff, dapper publisher of *Vogue*. He was a strong supporter of what she was up to with her candid-like fashion shots despite the disapproval not only of his artistic director, Agha, who felt that things had gotten out of hand, but also the magazine's readership. He ran a contest in *Vogue* in which two photographs were shown, one a studio study by Horst P. Horst of two models in evening gowns, leaning against a Directoire love seat, and on the page opposite, Toni Frissell's photograph of the two models in the same evening gowns outdoors on a beach. To Nast's surprise, three quarters of the public preferred the studio portraiture—very likely because showing evening clothes on a beach seemed artificial, indeed contrived. It was too much of a departure. Condé Nast, though nonplussed, stuck to his guns, and, of course, Toni did to hers.

As her reputation as a photographer flourished, so did her personal life. On a blind date with friends she met Francis McNeil Bacon III, a young Harvard graduate recently employed by a New York brokerage firm. As usual, Toni describes getting herself ready for their first date. "I went upstairs to dress and put on a pale lemon chiffon dress, a copy of a Vionnet, that had yards and yards of black satin sash. I dabbed some Callot Marriage d'Amour perfume behind my ears and doused my handkerchief with it. One more wisp of powder on my nose, and, oh yes, mother's double strand of pearls around

Toni Frissell with husband Mac Bacon, Medway Plantation, South Carolina, December 1961.

my neck. I put on the black satin ballet slippers, criss-crossed the ribbons and tied them around my ankles . . ."

Accompanied by another couple, Toni and Mac went downtown from the apartment and smuggled the champagne bottles (it was Prohibition) into a "cosily crowded" place called "El Chino's" in Greenwich Village. They danced. Toni, not surprisingly, made the first advance. "I turned my face to his cheek and tickled it with my eyelashes. The music stopped but we went on dancing for a few steps, reluctant to let each other go . . ."

The romance continued. Within a few months the two decided to get married and did so on September 9, 1932.

They remained close throughout their marriage, though often there was friction as Toni became increasingly intense about her photographic career. In many ways it became more important than her home life. She was away three quarters of the year. Their two children were brought up by a series of nannies. Toni once said about her absorption with photography that it was like being a movie actress . . . both losing themselves in the parts they play though on opposite sides of the camera.

When World War II started for the Americans on December 7, 1941, Toni wanted to become involved and, as might be expected, knew how to go about it. She persuaded Ovita Culp Hobby of the WACS to send her overseas to take pictures for the Red Cross. Her husband groaned and objected but to no avail. She flew to London. In her memoirs she writes of the barrage balloons in the sky, "It looked as though England were being held up by blimps."

She spent ten weeks covering Red Cross operations—"in field camps, from a stepladder at a Service Club dance to catch a conga chain as it went by . . . from a window to photograph the Scots Guards marching to the sound of their squirling bagpipes in the morning's mist . . . a Red Cross worker and a soldier standing awestruck in front of St. Paul's cathedral rising from the ruins."

She took a photograph of the damage a V-2 rocket had caused near Parliament Bridge—a "valley of destruction. At the edge half a brick house was torn apart, a bedroom with a white iron bed hanging out over the gap. The torn sheets were fluttering in the wind . . .

"As I turned the corner I stood riveted. A small boy was sitting at the bottom of a high pile of haphazard planks and beams. I was told he had come home from playing and found his house in shambles—his mother, father and brother dead under the rubble . . . he was looking up at the sky, his face an expression of both confusion and defiance."

Everywhere she went she snapped pictures. She had 250,000 flashbulbs shipped over from the United States. In a bombed-out church she arranged a picture with choirboys and American troops, which was published in *Life* magazine. Other publications took her work—*Collier's*, the *Saturday Evening*

Family dogs running
on the beach at
"Sherrewogue," Toni
Frissell's home
on Long Island.

Post. She was able to get an assignment to tour the European Theater of Operations covering the Eighth Air Force.

"When I broke the news to Mac and the children they didn't seem greatly surprised."

Toni went on to have a "busy" war. In Europe she persuaded authorities to let her fly in an artillery-spotting Piper Cub above the Hurtgen Forest and the scene of the Battle of the Bulge six weeks before. She was driving in a jeep near Grosshen when it was hit by shell fragments, some of them wounding the driver. She took pictures of a German tank covered with a sheen of phosphorous, a pair of legs sticking out of its turret.

She followed the Air Force down to Italy. She flew with the 332nd Fighter Pilot Squadron, an all-black detachment with the Fifteenth Air Force—going up in a Mustang P-51 flying cover for the Flying Fortresses returning from their mission north. As if her experiences with the Air Force were not enough, she finagled her way into the headquarters of an infantry division headquarters—the 10th Mountain. "I have friends in this division," she announced. "I would very much like to photograph their attack."

At a quieter time in Rome she photographed Pope Pius but with no less brazenness. She announced to a Vatican functionary, Count Galeazi, that "I am on this trip because I am one of the best photographers in America and although I am not a Catholic I would be most honored, etc. etc." The count caved in and arranged it.

"I knelt down and kissed his [the Pope's] beautiful ring. I noticed what long aesthetic fingers he had. He sat in a chair and I suggested he lean his elbow on a window sill and look out. He shook his head and said, 'No, that

Toni Frissell showing cameras to English children during World War II.

would not be correct.' I then photographed him sitting on his throne but the pictures weren't good because there was too much light reflected on his glasses. So I photographed him standing up as if he were looking out at the easter crowds . . ."

She went to Paris. She wrote: "Extraordinary to see a city still intact after the craters and skeleton ruins of London. But it was a strange, silent city . . . no sound of music, no sound of horns—the taxi horns which used to be such a part of Paris . . ."

It was on this trip that she met Ernest Hemingway, who had "liberated" the Hotel Ritz and was entertaining friends and hangers-on in *"chambre trente-et-un."* "He was standing by the door popping Perrier Jouet champagne corks." He led Toni to a red damask sofa. "That's enough popping corks." He began talking about Mary Welsh, the war correspondent who eventually became his wife. "Before that wonderful woman came along," he told Toni, "I loved being in the thick of battle. It was the juice of life. But Mary has changed everything. I've just received a dispatch from *Collier's* which wants me to return to my division at the front. I used to enjoy myself and had fun throwing grenades, but I believe I used up all my luck in the Hurtgen Forest. If I go on with the Allied rat-race and go once more to the Siegfried Line in the Mosel Valley I'll be killed. I'm afraid to go—not for myself but for Mary. Why is love so much stronger in war? I see myself dead

Toni Frissell and Major Roberts of the Red-Tailed Mustangs of the Fifteenth Air Force, 1945.

"When we touched down and swung the Plexiglas back, we asked the mechanic to take a picture of us with my camera. I set the speed with trembling hands. I looked more surprised than pleased—it had seemed as if we were traveling in a tight spiral faster than sound, and I was breathless."

beside a ditch and Mary, hearing the news, rushing to the front. I lie awake at night thinking of her looking for me . . . sometimes I think I'll quit and run away with Mary to a perfect Italian lake, the snow-mountains reflected in the water . . . One thing I'm sure of. My number is up . . . it's bad for a reporter to have battle-fatigue."

At this point in the somewhat morbid recitation, another bottle of champagne was uncorked, poured, and Hemingway's spirits, according to Toni, improved immeasurably.

Toni's work during the war was not limited to the general information magazines. Both the major fashion magazines, *Vogue* and *Harper's Bazaar*, had photographers covering the war. Toni was under contract to *Harper's Bazaar*. Representing *Vogue* was Lee Miller, a glamorous figure who had started her career in front of the cameras as a highly sought-after fashion model. In 1929 she went to Paris and apprenticed herself (and became the mistress of) the Surrealist artist and photographer Man Ray. Through him she met Jean Cocteau, who starred her in his classic 1930 film, *The Blood of a Poet*—a memorably visual role for which he covered her face with chalk-white pancake makeup and painted eyes on her closed eyelids.

When the war came, just as Toni adopted the Eighth Air Force, Miller became the official mascot of the 83rd Division in Europe. The two photographers were very much of a kind—energetic, enterprising. Marguerite

Toni Frissell with husband
Francis McNeil Bacon
in 1940.

Higgins, the *New York Herald*'s war correspondent, once complained to Miller, "How is it when I arrive to cover a story you are just leaving?"

Miller was a fine writer as well, augmenting her pictures with vivid texts, and often setting up scenes she thought would amuse her readers: when the Allies entered Munich she had a friend take a picture of her in Hitler's bathtub; she then went down the street to Eva Braun's villa and slept in her bed. There on a bedside table she noticed a phone marked Berchtesgaden, Hitler's hideout in the mountains; she put through a call. No answer, but good copy.

One might guess that a lively rivalry could have sprung up between the two women war correspondents, but Toni Frissell's main difficulty was not with Lee Miller, but rather with an annoying presence in the home office—Louise Dahl-Wolfe. With *Harper's Bazaar* since 1936, Dahl-Wolfe was one of the pioneers in the use of daylight lighting for fashion photography; her portraits were highly stylized, inevitably suggesting that an editor or a designer was on hand to tell the models exactly what to do against backgrounds that were often replicas of stage sets, Moorish castles, archways, swimming pools. Her work during the war years was "home front" studies—Five-Star mothers, a young woman in a negligee kneeling in front of a fireplace staring into the flames, presumably thinking of her fiancé at the front. She was a short stout woman who stood on a box to peer through the viewfinder of her portrait cameras—the antithesis of the thin-shanked models she was photographing. Not surprisingly, she was envious of Toni's quite glamorous lifestyle and certainly of her work. She bluntly stated that she would quit if Toni's photographs appeared in *Harper's Bazaar*. This forced Carmel Snow, back at *Bazaar*, to return Toni's war pictures and the photograph she had taken of the pope. Nothing would dissuade Dahl-Wolfe, even when assured that none of Toni's fashion spreads would be published in *Bazaar*, only her war pictures: Snow pleaded it was essential that Toni should be kept on because the magazine would lose its war correspondent. Dahl-Wolfe's reply was that she would quit if *anything* of Toni's appeared in the magazine. Actually, this peremptory behavior seems very much in character: Dahl-Wolfe left *Harper's Bazaar* in 1958 when the new art director was presumptuous enough to step up and look through the camera at what she was photographing. "This has never happened in all my years," she said. After a short stint with *Vogue*, she retired to the country. "A difficult bird," she was described to me.

It was not until the war was over, with Toni back in the States and given such comparatively tame assignments as photographing debutantes and their events that the differences between the various parties were smoothed over.

In 1950, *Harper's Bazaar* sent Toni on an assignment to England that Dahl-Wolfe might well have envied. It was to photograph a social study of the English: *we speak the same language but do we* look *alike?*

London was quite changed from what Toni remembered from the war years: "Hydrangeas bloomed in the newly-painted green window boxes. The Hyde Park flotillas of nannies pushed their young charges under the green leafy trees. On Oxford Street, tall, slim men, wearing toppers, walked in pale grey striped trousers. Music was in the air—the military bands of the Changing of the Guard, the hurdy-gurdy clanging like a pianola at the end of Upper Brook Street; the noon-time music of the Hungarian orchestra at Claridge's as I registered and checked into my room. At night the soft sound of dance music wafted in from open windows. In the long English twilight, debutantes in tulle dresses floated from the doors of their chauffeur-driven cars . . ."

Toni photographed state funerals, balls, house parties, the Bamaer Games in Scotland ("the Queen had on a pale blue tweed suit and off-the-face hat so people could see her. What beautiful blue eyes . . . but when I came to Princess Elizabeth with my camera she put on her 'boot face' which was her name for being cross"), grouse shoots, country dances, the coming-of-age party for Lord Carnegie when he became the Duke of Fife—the guests leaving at dawn and seeing the bonfires burning on the surrounding hills in celebration of the young peer coming into his inheritance . . .

Her eye as a photographer is often matched by the prose of her memoir. On a visit to Eton on the fourth of June, the day that the boys' school commemorates their founder, Henry VI, she writes: "Flocks of parents arrive—mothers in flowery garden-party dresses, white gloves and wide-brimmed picture hats trimmed with roses, fathers in grey toppers and morning coats, younger sisters in dancing-class dresses, their hair tied back with narrow satin ribbons the same color as the dress . . . Families drive up to the edge of the cricket field in their Rolls-Royces (many), Daimlers, Triumphs, MGs, and Morrises. When the morning play is over, they open the back trunk, pull out a steamer rug and a wicker hamper basket, a bucket of iced champagne, and they picnic in the grass behind their car. It is easy to tell class distinction by the type of car. There are so many sights to be photographed that are different from American school outings: the vicar (or is he a bishop?) striding down a path underneath the blooming horse chestnut trees in his black gaiters, buttoned up the side, and his hat turned up at the side, his wife trailing a respectful distance behind . . . a younger brother and sister sitting on the bench watching the cricket match, the boy rigidly erect, his top hat squarely on top of his head, she, her ankles demurely crossed, one patent leather shoe on, the other off . . . a young girl and her beau sitting under a tree feeding her sleek, fawn-colored whippets smoked-salmon sandwiches (I bet the dogs were sick) . . . a family by the river picnicking in a large punt, the boys in Eton collars and rolled-up shirt sleeves eating strawberries and cream from plates . . . a grandmother sitting on a bench under a flowering chestnut tree, despite the shade her parasol held erect.

"It was interesting to listen to the babble of different languages," she writes. "I particularly noticed Englishmen's voices—the 'no really!' and 'how extraordinary!' said often in high constipated voices. When we Americans disapprove of something, we are apt to say, 'It stinks!', whereas an Englishman says, 'How extraordinary!' They mean the same thing."

A great hope was realized during this trip. Visiting Blenheim Palace as a guest of the Duke and Duchess of Marlborough she got a chance to photograph Winston Churchill, who had come for lunch. Toni sat facing, as she put it, "that glorious bulldog." She found him shorter than she expected, but his "noble forehead" gave an effect of height. She writes: "In repose he had two sides to his face. The right hand corner of his mouth turned up slightly; on the left he looked dour. Most powerful men have two sides to their face.

"When lunch was over, the ladies left the gentlemen to the brandy and cigars. Mary [the duchess] took me over to the piano and showed me the pictures I had taken of her children in the surf off the Vanderbilt estate in Florida. I remembered how uneasy I had been that the Vanderbilts would catch me using my camera on their beach. Now that picture turned out to stand me in good stead.

" 'Get up and get your Kodak,' Mary said. 'I will persuade Winston to let you take a snap.'

"At the very idea my heart fluttered.

"I went up to my room and collected my Rolliflex loaded with Tri-X film, twelve exposures. I always bring two identically loaded cameras, but this time I left one upstairs as I well expected Churchill would only sit for twelve exposures.

"Then I knelt down. 'Please let me take a good picture of this man of destiny. This is the most important picture I will ever take. Help me dear God!'

"Down in the sitting room Churchill had come in. He was in a high good humor, puffing contentedly on a cigar.

"Mary said to him, 'Winston, Toni Frissell is a very good photographer. She took that picture of the children on the piano. Would you let her take a snap of you?'

"I thought 'Oh dear, not just one snap. It takes a couple of exposures to get a good likeness.'

Toni Frissell entering
10 Downing Street
to photograph
Churchill before the
Coronation, 1953.

" 'Delighted, my dear,' he said. 'Where would you like me to sit?' "

Toni records that when the session actually started, Churchill became "rather frigid."

"First he made a series of V for Victory signs as if I was in a crowd of newspaper photographers. Presently an impatient look came over his face. I was up to nine exposures and hadn't accomplished anything. In my mind I tried to think of an appropriate thing to say. Finally I burst out with what was on my mind. 'Mr. Churchill,' I said desperately. 'You are not thinking the right thoughts'—this to one of the great thinkers of the century!

" 'Oh,' he said.

"I went on. 'You are thinking how tiresome this woman is who's detaining you when you want to go out for a walk with Mrs. Churchill. Are those the right thoughts for this struggling photographer who wants to record a great picture of you?'

"I said this with a broad smile and in my most persuasive voice. At those outrageous words the boredom and impatience left Churchill's face. He looked gentle with just a quiver of a smile on the right side of his mouth. The remaining three frames were taken with all the speed that a $\frac{1}{10}$ of a second exposure would permit. I knew I had three."

The photographs turned out as she hoped. Indeed, when she showed the proofs to Mrs. Churchill, she was told, " 'These are very fine. Winston will be so pleased. I have never seen anyone catch a better likeness. They are the perfect portraits of an elder statesman. I would like to make one of them his official portrait.'

" 'Oh, Mrs. Churchill!' I said, stunned. 'What about the great picture taken by Karsh before the Canadian Conference.'

" 'Never,' said Mrs. Churchill firmly. 'I will not have that picture in my house. When Karsh pulled the cigar out of my husband's mouth he showed a world statesman a great discourtesy. I will have nothing to do with Karsh or his pictures.' "

Toni disagreed with Mrs. Churchill's assessment of perhaps the most famous photo-portrait of her husband. "Karsh is a great photographer," she writes in her memoir, "and took a wonderful defiant picture at a time, during the war, when defiance was important; it is a pity that this method was so publicized."

Harper's Bazaar published her English photographs. Soon after, very much in the common if curious tradition of shifting allegiance from one fashion magazine to another, Toni went over to *Vogue*. This followed what she refers to as the "Kennedy episode." *Harper's Bazaar* had sent her to take photographs at one of the most glittering social events of the fifties—the wedding reception after Jacqueline Bouvier's marriage to Senator John F. Kennedy in Newport, Rhode Island. It was not an easy assignment. She found it difficult to get the newlyweds away from the wedding guests—a large number of them Kennedys. "There are so many of them and they are so vital: they are bound to take over any place like a swarm of locusts." Finally Toni was able to get them out on a stretch of lawn at Hammersmith Farm with its view of the sea. "They walked out together and I suggested they face each other from a distance and hold hands looking into each other's eyes. A slight breeze came up and blew the veil behind her. How did I know I was photographing such people of destiny?"

There were others who didn't guess either. When Toni reached New York after the ceremony, she received a call from Carmel Snow, who said she had no use for the pictures. "Don't bother to send them. I don't want to see them. There's been such notoriety they are worthless to *Harper's Bazaar*."

When the magazine refused to pay for her work, even her expenses, Toni left the publication in a "high dudgeon." Since *Vogue* was upset with her because she had worked for a rival, Toni found herself in a "sort of photographic hiatus." Fortunately, she was losing interest in fashion work. "It seems altogether too unrealistic today with the models looking more like architectural designs than human beings."

On the condition that she could be relieved of taking fashion shots, she was finally persuaded to return to *Vogue*. To her delight, one of her first assignments was to return to England for the Coronation in the spring of 1953. In her memoir she recalls "the flags, the pennants, streamers, banners, and bunting with the coats of arms hanging from noble buildings. Berkeley Square, I remember, had lanterns hanging from the trees and a mechanical nightingale singing in the branches."

One day during Coronation Week she received a call from Lady Churchill, who asked her to come to 10 Downing Street after the ceremonies and photograph Sir Winston in his Order of the Garter robes along with other members of the family.

" 'Yes,' I said in a choked voice."

Toni was so nervous that when she arrived and was offered tea, "my hand rattled the royal blue and gold-flowered Davenport china so I could hardly drink it. When it was time to do the photograph, he stood to one side adjusting his velvet garter coat. Lady Churchill was hanging the 'Big George' over his neck—a miniature 18-karat statue of St. George on horseback killing the dragon. He had been loaned the 'Big George' by the Duke of Wellington for Coronation Day. Then he put on a black velvet Garter hat with a wide brim and a swinging white ostrich plume that tickled his neck. But somehow it made him look like a baby in a perambulator. I lost his noble brow. When he sat down I suggested he hold his hat as he looked more like 'a man of destiny' that way. After removing his hat he looked at me quizzically. I caught that expression. However, it wasn't long before he looked impatient and I got the usual bulldog expression."

In the memoir Toni lists some of the tips she used for such portrait sessions:

1. Catch the subject at an instant of pleasure or emotion
2. Know your subject's interests beforehand . . . this so you can get him or her talking, even to the point of saying something provocative to the extent of outrageousness
3. Click your camera at typewriter speed. Film is a cheap commodity
4. Luck—the commodity that puts one at a crucial event and the chance is given of recording a vital instant

At this stage of her career Toni left the fashion magazines entirely and went to work for the new Time-Life publication *Sports Illustrated*. It was exhilarating work and she went at it with typical and often unnerving enthusiasm. In Unionville, Pennsylvania, she hired a helicopter to photograph a foxhunt. "All hell broke loose below. Horses reared into gardens, unseating their riders; hounds went cowering under the horses, and one lady was thrown from her sidesaddle . . ."

Wherever Toni was assigned, her presence was often felt with dire results. John Steinbeck, visiting in Barbados, made the mistake of telling her that he enjoyed "watching the hermit crabs at the bottom of my pier in Sag Harbor, Long Island." This innocent observation instantly prompted Toni to exclaim: "Great! Let's go aqualunging this afternoon. Meet you at three o'clock." It turned out the famous novelist knew nothing about what he was being propelled to do, and indeed had to be rescued from the depths of the ocean and given mouth-to-mouth resuscitation. "Steinbeck came to with a snort. It was a close call."

There seemed no end to Toni's assignments. The home from which she set out on such expeditions was a lovely seventeenth-century house renovated by Stanford White. Located in St. James, Long Island, it was named Sherrewogue, an Indian name which means "across the water"—a name which her children joked about and said it meant "where their mother was." Toni's daughter was asked in her early years her mother's whereabouts. "Probably in Africa or somewhere," she replied. "Oh well, she will return."

Her son, Varick, was apparently of the same opinion. In a boyhood essay he writes:

> My father is a stock broker. Thats not so bad but you couldn't guese what my mother is. She should lieve the picture taking to the men. The only thing I like about it is the money she gets for it, sometimes makes more than three hundred dollars on one pictor. The only thing I cant see is how she gets around to so many places. She been to South America Afirca Texas England Honlue and a great many other places but she never gets tired of taking pictures. Its really quite amazing. Sometimes she has good idies. One day she had this crazy idea of bringing a camel here to the house but the camel had a corld or something and couldnt come. Most of the time she had modeles here or something like that. Id never like to be a phortagrafer, thats one thing.

Perhaps to compensate for being constantly away from home Toni photographed her two children to illustrate Robert Louis Stevenson's *A Child's Garden of Verses*. She never tried to pose them, but relied entirely on photographing them when they struck the right attitudes. Children, she once said, are the easiest people in the world to photograph. "Their movements are natural, their expressions unstudied, and they're quick to tell you when they've had enough. I personally prefer to take them in a serious or angry mood, or extremely gay."

Toni also noted that friends eating was a good time to take pictures, because they tended to be "natural" doing so. Hence she took an enormous number of pictures at picnics—combining her love of *plein air* photography and her subjects *aux tables*.

Always, she was under constant demand to photograph the famous. One day Mike Todd, the famous showman then married to Elizabeth Taylor, called.

> Todd: I want you to come at once and photograph Liz and our six-week old daughter, Liza.

Toni: I can't. I'm photographing Eisenhower.

Todd: Who's that? Well, come next week. I'll send my plane for you.

Mike Todd promised her a gondola in return. This never materialized. Instead, after the shoot he offered some rather gratuitous advice: "You must walk into every room as if onto a stage. Do it with authority."

One of Toni's last projects was to photograph the "distinguished old ladies of America" for *Life*. From childhood she had always been fascinated by such sights as a "great white-haired lady sitting erect in her diamond dog collar, peering through her lorgnette." Each of her subjects in the *Life* assignment had to be over seventy years old, involved in important causes, and with big families they dominated. Among those who sat for her were Mrs. Nicholas Longworth (who asked her to notice the top of her head, which was bald, and which President Johnson kissed when she came to dine at the White House), Mrs. Harper Sibley, Mrs. Malcolm Peabody, and a next-door neighbor in Long Island, Mrs. Christopher Temple Emmet. The last named was a favorite subject. Toni photographed her in her ninety-fourth year. "Everyone in her vast family trembled at the tap of her gold-headed cane. Nobody dared disobey her summons, be it morning, noon, or night. Often the summons would occur at 3 A.M. as she couldn't sleep and wished to play dominoes beside her bed. Her wish was law. I brought my small Italian whippet with me because I thought he would add to the picture's style. Greyhounds were often represented in royal medieval tapestries. She was seated on a velvet settee beneath a full-length painting of herself at eighteen—I think by Sargent—sitting in the same settee. I settled Bambi on a cushion. My photograph fell together. She had the look of a powerful eagle. Her long fingers grasped the gold-headed cane and made her look as though she were stretching toward someone. Her profile was edged with a soft light. Today she spoke softly. Bambi, curled up on the satin pillow, fell asleep."

When the picture of Mrs. Emmet appeared in *Life*, Mrs. Emmet was shown it after recovering from an illness. Toni writes, "Her grandson told me that she opened her eyes and looked at it. 'Oh, what an excellent picture of Pope John,' she murmured. She was very Catholic."

The descriptions of her sessions with the great ladies ends Toni's memoir. The last lines of the manuscript read, "Today my friends come up to me and ask, 'Are you still taking pictures?'

" 'No. I am writing about all of you.' "

Of course, this stopped too. But the legacy is left. In 1961 Toni had a show

Toni Frissell with son
Varick at a church window
on Long Island, 1944.

At "Sherrewogue" in 1980.
Photograph by Brent Brookfield
Loyer, her granddaughter.

sponsored by IBM which was entitled "The World Is So Full of a Number of Things." In the catalog she wrote a statement that stands for her attitude about a career in photography. "In this show I have tried to capture a number of things I have seen around me, at work and on holidays, a child's world of discovery. My own varied fields of travel, ways of life, both simple and splendid, and on my assignment in the European Theater in World War II. Here also are moments of relaxation as well as of achievement. And most of all, human faces I have found memorable. If they are not as happy as kings, it is because in this imperfect world and these hazardous times, the camera eye, like the eye of a child, often sees true . . ."

— GEORGE PLIMPTON

The italicized passages that follow are taken from the writings of Toni Frissell.

Toni Frissell

PHOTOGRAPHS: 1933–1967

Mrs. C. Ruckelshaus, New York.
Vogue, February 1938.

Fashion

Vogue, August 1935.

"I took my first fashion photograph in 1931. Until then, fashion pictures had always been done in a studio. But I was never mechanically minded with lights and exposures, so I decided to go outside on location to photograph models with their hair blowing in the wind. As my skills grew I took my camera and models to Peru, to Jamaica, to Guatemala and the West Indies—always seeking out natural settings.

"In all modesty I must say that this changed the whole style of fashion photography from that time onward."

Model Sydney Kraus at Marineland, Florida.
Vogue, December 1939.

Tryall Plantation, Jamaica.
Harper's Bazaar, October 1948.

Peru.
Harper's Bazaar, January 1952.

Vogue, January 1939.

Vogue, November 1940.

LEFT:
Sculling off Jamaica.
Harper's Bazaar, October 1948.

Mrs. Douglas Burden surf casting.
Vogue, May 1938.

Vogue, June 1938.

Vogue, May 1942.

White pigeons in dovecote
at St. James, Long Island, February 1961.

RIGHT:
Dolphin tank, Marineland, Florida.
Vogue, October 1939.

Vogue, August 1944.

Vogue, June 1940.

Harper's Bazaar, February 1950.

LEFT:
Harper's Bazaar, August 1949.

Harper's Bazaar, July 1951.

Bikini-clad model Dovima, Montego Bay, Jamaica.
Harper's Bazaar, May 1947.

"Model Dovima was dressed in the first bikini to be seen away from France.
Next to the Casablanca was a tall white diving platform up fifty feet. I called to
the fisherman and asked if he would let my model pose below the diving board.
The effect was remarkable. The picture won an art award the next year."

Harper's Bazaar, 1948.

Model Evelyn Tripp on the steps of the Lincoln Memorial, Washington,
D.C., 1954. This advertisement for Garfinckel's department store appeared
in many fashion magazines.

RIGHT:
Harper's Bazaar, February 1947.

2 4

Bermuda, June 1945.

LEFT:
Harper's Bazaar, January 1950.

"Crazy with the heat."
Vogue, July 1937.

RIGHT:
Toni Frissell's daughter Sidney as "Alice in Wonderland,"
Medway Plantation, South Carolina, 1947.

Victoria Station, London.
Harper's Bazaar, 1951.

American soldier, Red Bull Regiment, Italy, Easter Sunday, 1945.

"We went to another scene on a green hill covered with flowers:
hyacinth, yellow and pink primroses. One man was carefully decorating
camouflage on his tin hat with flowers stuck in the netting mesh.
What an Easter bonnet."

War

Boy with shaven head in children's prison.

"The worst part of war, in my opinion, is what happens to the survivors—the widows without home or family, the ragged kids left to wander as orphans. I saw many of these in wartime Europe: a young British boy sitting by the rubble of the home where his parents lay buried shortly after a V-2 had hit; youngsters with shaven heads in a children's prison; human mascots, adopted by army units that had then moved on, leaving the children to fend for themselves. The aftereffects of war are never pretty to see. Neither should they be forgotten."

Abandoned child, Battersea, England, January 1945.

At the Swedish-American Line pier, New York.
Harper's Bazaar, November 1949.

Graveyard, 1945.

German prisoners of war taken by the 10th Mountain Division,
Monte Belvedere, Italy, spring 1945.

*"Our guide, a captain, took us to a house where they were screening
German prisoners of war. They had large tags around their necks
reading 'Prisoner of War.' Three of them had farmer's faces, and one
looked like a former Hitler Youth. All of them had a terrible look of
disillusionment on their faces."*

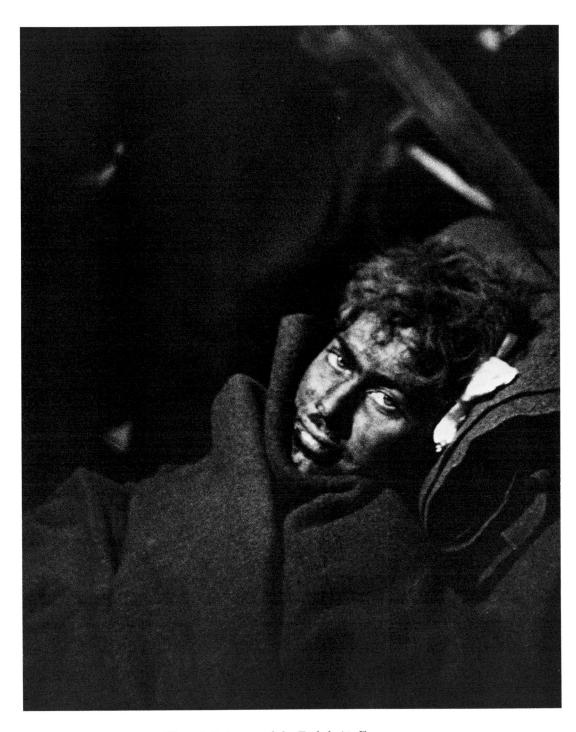

Wounded airman of the Eighth Air Force,
Pinetree, England, January 1945.

Italy, 1945.

Eighth Air Force briefing room, Pinetree, England, January 1945.

"The crews look first at the map, then turn away with whistles of disapproval. Someone says: 'Here we go, right up flack alley.' Another: 'I'd rather go to Brooklyn.' They are worried now, the sleepiness leaves their eyes. Apprehension takes its place, for their mission is no picnic. A dog trots into the room, sniffs around one of the pilot's feet. The pilot absentmindedly picks him up, but never takes his eyes off the wall."

The Siegfried Line, Rhône Valley, early spring 1945.

"Ahead of us were soldiers walking up the road ten feet apart.
We were requested to get out of the jeep and walk separately.
We were on a very exposed part of the road—and easy targets,
like ducks in a shooting gallery, apparently in full
view of the enemy."

The Siegfried Line, Rhône Valley, 1945.

"A soldier with a two-day-old stubble on his chin was propped up against a plank clasping a tommy gun. Was he dead tired or was he just plain dead?"

Old woman chestnut seller reading of
Franklin D. Roosevelt's death, Italy, April 1945.

Red Cross worker with wounded soldier, England, 1942.
Vogue.

*"About ten weeks ago I returned from England, where I made an extensive
photographic tour for the American Red Cross. I saw Red Cross field directors who
live with the army and take down the boys' case histories so as not to worry their
wives and families back home. I went to hospitals and saw and photographed the
wonderful job the Red Cross recreation workers are doing—writing letters, playing
cards and games, reading—thus keeping up the morale of the wounded soldiers. To
have served this organization was a privilege. I hope that some of the two thousand
pictures I took will make people realize what a great job the Red Cross is doing."*

Boy sitting in the rubble of his home where his parents lie buried after a
V-2 bomb hit, London, January 1945.

*"I was told he had come back from playing and found his house a shambles—
his mother, father and brother dead under the rubble . . . he was looking up at the
sky, his face an expression of both confusion and defiance. The defiance made him
look like a young Winston Churchill. This photograph was used by IBM to publicize
a show in London. The boy grew up to become a truck driver after the war, and
walking past the IBM offices, he recognized his picture."*

The homeless victims of war, London, 1945.

Two youngsters in children's prison.

Berlin Wall, October 1961.

"Before I left Mac for Berlin he said, 'You can go on this assignment but don't dare go near the wall.' Of course, I did. On the second day I saw a remarkable picture. I stopped the car. There was a West Berliner in uniform smiling at me, with an East German on the other side with a gun. After I developed the picture, I saw the horrible East Berliner pointing the machine gun at my lens. We read in the paper the next day that a photographer had been shot the day before."

LEFT:
Berlin, October 1961.
Saturday Review, October 1967.

Red-Tailed Mustangs' briefing room.

"The 332nd Fighter Pilot Squadron was an all-black outfit of the Fifteenth Air Force, commanded by a remarkable leader, Colonel Benjamin Davis. At the briefing, intelligence officers warned the pilots to take cyanide if they were forced down and captured by the Ustachi, wild tribesmen in the mountains of Yugoslavia. They were a cruel, ruthless group of people who tortured their captives in a manner far worse than the Gestapo."

LEFT:
Ground crewman of the Red-Tailed Mustangs, 332nd Fighter Pilot
Squadron, the all-black outfit of the Fifteenth Air Force, Italy, March 1945.

Love

Baron Guy de Rothschild and his wife Marie-Hélène,
February 1961.

"What is it?

"How does one define it?

"I have always been curious about this elusive subject.

"I've tried to convey a few of my own observations of love, and
its different forms and moods . . ."

LEFT:
Lovers along the Seine, Paris, March 1964.

Alida Lessard with her daughter Laura, granddaughter
and great-granddaughter of Stanford White, June 1963.

RIGHT:
Mrs. John Huston and her daughter Angelica, March 1959.

The Duke and Duchess of Windsor, Palm Beach,
May 1950.

RIGHT:
Doris and Yul Brynner, Florida, April 1962.

Lovers near the Thames, London, 1962.

RIGHT:
Elizabeth Taylor, Mike Todd, and their infant daughter Liza,
September 1957. *Life.*

"Liza was six weeks old and not yet a camera star. She screamed bloody murder until someone brought her a bottle. She bubbled and burped over Liz's shoulder, and then threw up all over her dress and Liz's Austrian puffed-sleeve blouse. Exit two stars. I suggested that Liza be brought down nude, with Liz in a strapless top. Mike: 'My daughter in the nude? Nothin' doin'.' But Mike brought down Liza as requested—nude— and laid her down beside her mother. Liz had a minimum of makeup, and I could see it come clearly through that she adored this child and Mike. Liza was falling asleep, though she turned her face, eyes closed, toward my camera. Mike leaned over Liz's head to see this little red miracle they had created. Dear Mike, he was responsible for one of the great pictures I have taken."

Toni Frissell's son Varick Bacon in "Wintertime"
in *A Child's Garden of Verses*.

Children

Toni Frissell's granddaughter Brent Brookfield Loyer, May 1963.

"In our household there have always been children—and consequently birthday parties, puppet shows, tea on the lawn, and wonderful opportunities to dress up the girls in Edwardian clothes from our attic. Just as I love children, I love to preserve these old-fashioned souvenirs of a vanishing splendor."

Coco the poodle walking down the streets of New York.
Life, December 1949.

"I want to go home." Courchevel, France, March 1964.

John Scully, future founder of Apple computers, St. James, Long Island, 1946.

"They managed to lure Johnny Scully from across the road into an old dusty stage coach
standing in the vacated barn. 'Come here, Johnny, we have something to show you.'
Johnny, being a polite redheaded little boy, followed them and climbed up to the door,
opening it and going in. Sidney and her friend opened the dark, dusty door and looked in
at him. 'Look, John, do you see what we see?' Slam, lock, went the door. 'John, what do
you see in there? Do you see black widow spiders?' Predictably, Sidney's story was a
little different: 'John and I did play in the old coach, but I never locked him in. I played
the Queen and John the Prince, since he was two years younger. A friend and I did,
however, lock John in a stable with one of the quieter horses, scaring him to death.' "

Portugal, 1946.

LEFT:
St. Augustine, Florida, 1939.

Linda and Pam Peyton at Caroline Church,
Setauket, New York, June 1958.

LEFT:
"Autumn Fires" from *A Child's Garden of Verses.*

Vermont, September 1960.

Long Island Sound, 1957.

On the beach, July 1947.

"My Shadow" from *A Child's Garden of Verses*.

"For a long time I'd been casting around in my mind's eye for a book of poetry to illustrate with photographs. What better book than Robert Louis Stevenson's."

Toni Frissell's daughter Sidney on the cover of *A Child's Garden of Verses*.

" 'The world is so full of a number of things, / I'm sure we should all be as happy as kings.' Or so I thought as I marshaled our children Varick and Sidney and their friend through a series of Robert Louis Stevenson poems. I endeavored to make my picture taking a game. I directed the children to march through fields of daisies, I put Sidney in a raincoat and an umbrella on a shiny pavement in a pelting rainstorm for the poem 'Rain, Rain, Go Away,' and I swung her up in the sky so blue until her face became slightly green."

Natalie White, Stanford White's great-granddaughter,
Long Island, June 1963.

Stephanie White, another of Stanford White's great-granddaughters,
Long Island, August 1957.

Frederic Koltay with dog Winston,
May 1957.

Gertrude Legendre's springer spaniel on a leopard-skin rug
(a trophy from an African safari) at Medway Plantation,
South Carolina, December 1961.

Vermont, 1960:
"We should all be as happy as kings."

Toni Frissell's grandson Montgomery Brookfield, drinking ginger ale, 1963.

RIGHT:
Trevor Huxley in a barn on the Stanford White estate, "Box Hill,"
May 1961.

"When you're a mother, a grandmother, and a photographer, as I am, you are fortunate. You never lack subjects for your camera. Children are actually the easiest people in the world to photograph: their movements are natural, their expressions unstudied, and they're quick to tell you when they've had enough."

Blenheim Palace, the family seat of the Dukes of Marlborough, 1950.

Harper's Bazaar.

Sir Winston Churchill in his robes of the Order of the Garter on Coronation Day, 1953.
Vogue.

"The door of 10 Downing Street opened and I dashed upstairs with my assistant with more dignity than I felt. I was getting the usual butterflies in my solar plexus. I walked into the long room. The younger generation was letting off steam, turning somersaults. Young Winston was dressed as a page. He was sitting with dignity, having a cup of tea. Sir Winston put on a black velvet Garter hat with a wide brim and a swinging white ostrich plume that tickled his neck. Somehow it made him look like a baby in a perambulator. I lost his noble brow. So when he sat down, I asked that he hold his hat, as he would look more 'the man of destiny.' After that remark, he removed his hat, but he looked at me quizzically. I caught that expression."

Nannies in the park, London, 1963.

RIGHT:
The Honorable Reginald Wynn, London, 1950.
Harper's Bazaar.

The Duke of Marlborough after the Coronation service,
London, June 1953.

*"I saw Bert Marlborough—still in his coronet, trimmed with strawberry
leaves and all its regalia—smoking a big fat cigar. A close-up was
too good to miss."*

Sir Winston Churchill's grandchildren leaving the birthday party of his
granddaughter Emma Soames, London, 1953.

*"As the guests left Eaton Square, I caught another picture that would be seen nowhere
but London—the prim nannies in their stiff hats and tailored coats and the children in
their equally tailored coats, who skipped along at their nannies' sides holding their
floating balloons by their strings."*

RIGHT:
The Honorable Charles Spencer-Churchill, youngest child of the Duke and
Duchess of Marlborough, at Blenheim Palace.
Harper's Bazaar, September 1950.

"Charles Spencer-Churchill is the youngest child of the Duke and Duchess of Marlborough, and a nephew of Winston Churchill. His school days are spent at Summerfield,
preparing for Eton, and his holidays at the family seat, Blenheim Palace, in Oxfordshire.
Footnote to the times: When Blenheim was thrown open to visitors recently, and the Duke
and Duchess showed people about, Charles set up a booth, autographed his old toys, and
sold them to the highest bidder. With the proceeds he squired his nanny to a film." —
Harper's Bazaar.

Michael Astor family
in front of Bruen Abbey, England, 1953.

John Jacob Astor children
at Hatley Park, England, 1953.

Harper's Bazaar, July 1950.

Lord Hailey, Coronation Day, London, 1953.

"There was one lord in particular who attracted my lens's attention. He stood in the middle of the street, his robes gathered around him like wings out of the wet—white knee breeches, white stockings, black buckled shoes. Like a stork looking through silver-rimmed glasses, he was Lord Hailey, and he was oblivious to my camera."

The Duchess of Marlborough in her Coronation robes
at Blenheim Palace, Coronation Day, 1953.

*"The Duchess of Marlborough stood up between the Doric columns looking toward the main
entrance of Blenheim Palace. As she looked out, she shook her head in wonder and said, 'What a
folly.' Her Coronation robe was a white satin gown heavily encrusted with gold embroidery; the red
velvet cape that hung from her shoulders was trimmed all around with white ermine and black tails.
A diamond tiara glistened in her white-streaked auburn hair. She had long kid gloves that reached
her shoulders, and she held in her hands the small coronet with the velvet top edged with ermine
and gold strawberry leaves. The strawberry leaves signified that this was the crown of a duchess. At
the moment the Archbishop of Canterbury crowns the new Queen, all the realm stand up, holding
their crowns over their heads. The men are then to put them on."*

Lady Churchill at Hyde Park Gate
on her seventy-eighth birthday, 1963.
Saturday Review.

*"I believe Lady Churchill is one of the most beautiful women
I ever photographed."*

Sir Winston Churchill at Blenheim, 1950.
This photograph was used as his official portrait.

*" 'Mr. Churchill, you are not thinking the right thoughts. . . . You are
thinking how tiresome this woman is who's detaining you when you want to
go out for a walk with Mrs. Churchill. Are those the right thoughts for this
struggling photographer who wants to record a great photograph of you?' I
said with a broad smile and my most persuasive voice. At those outrageous
words the boredom and impatience left Churchill's face. He looked gentle,
with just a quiver of a smile on the right side of his mouth."*

Brother and sister at cricket match at Eton, June 1950.
Harper's Bazaar.

Lord Albemarle at Londonderry House, London, 1950.

Sport

OVERLEAF:
Cubbing at dawn, Unionville.
Sports Illustrated, October 1954.

"The season was early September, and I stayed with Nancy Hannum, who was master of the Plunkett Stewart Hounds. A September mist lay all over the valley. As we climbed the steep hill, we came out of the fog into the bright sunlight. Below we saw the hounds, and Nancy in a white linen cubbing coat and button-up gaiters. We could see the fog thick in every valley. This combination of early-morning fog and sunlight was a natural for a beautiful photograph. This picture has been used in a number of exhibitions, and hung on Mr. [Henry] Luce's office wall."

LEFT:
Horses and cattle at dawn, King Ranch, Texas, 1943.
From *The King Ranch, 1939–1944: A Photographic Essay.*

The Meath Hunt, Ireland. Whips Dodo Dunne and David Durnew
take hounds across the river.
Sports Illustrated, November 1956.

Cubbing at Unionville, Pennsylvania, October 1953.

Sports Illustrated.

Skiing at Monte Rosa glacier, Switzerland, April 1957.
From left: guide Elias Julen, Laura Leonard Ault, Sylvia Coe, and guide Paul Julen.

"Because of crevasses, skiers had to be roped together. The guides took their poles and tied them to their rucksacks so that each skier could take up or let out the rope according to speed. A guide led the way and a second guide was the last man on the rope, to secure the party in case someone fell into a crevasse. The snow was terrible—all breakable crust the whole way—but the run was great fun and a challenge."

Climbers, Zermatt, Switzerland.
Sports Illustrated, July 1955.

Cutting a calf from the herd.
From *The King Ranch.*

*"When a cut-out calf heads for the brush, the race is on.
Sometimes the calf wins, but only temporarily."*

Clamming at dusk, St. James, Long Island, 1944.

LEFT:
The Earl of Cadogan in action at the
Blenheim Pheasant Drive, England, 1956.
Sports Illustrated, 1957.

The King Ranch, Texas, December 1967.
From *The King Ranch.*

Surf casting, Nantucket, August 1957.

Duck hunter setting out decoys, California, 1959.
Sports Illustrated.

RIGHT:
The Matterhorn, Zermatt, Switzerland.

Fox hunter smoking, Unionville, November 1949.

LEFT:
Hunter and doves, Medway Plantation, South Carolina,
December 1953.

Dawn on the Oklahoma Track, Saratoga, New York, 1963.

Famous horse breeder Ambrose Clark.
Vogue, October 1953.

Foxhounds before the hunt, November 1956.
Sports Illustrated.

Foxhounds at the end of a hunt,
Unionville, 1953.

"Mr. and Mrs. Morgan Wing of Millbrook, New York.
Mr. Wing is master of the Sandamona Beagle Pack."

Harper's Bazaar, September 1952.

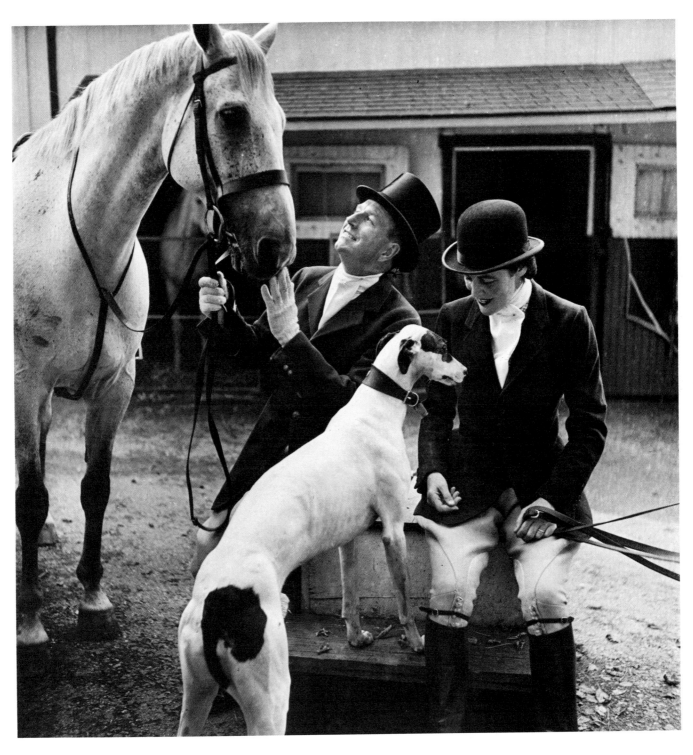

Mr. and Mrs. Edgar Scott, 1949.

Ticker tape parade for presidential candidate Richard M. Nixon,
New York, November 1960.

Photojournalism

President Franklin D. Roosevelt,
Camp Oglethorpe, Chattanooga, Tennessee, 1943.

"The story of my life is told in terms of photographs I have taken, places I have visited, and people I have met. This is as it should be. A photographer keeps a biographical record with every new assignment, and the photographer's subjects help shape her destiny."

South Carolina, December 1962.

RIGHT:
New Orleans, December 1962.

Port Arthur, Texas, November 1962. From a photographic essay
commissioned by Gulf Oil for their annual report.

Coast Guard Auxiliary, August 1957.

Jamaica, 1948.

Calypso player at Round Hill,
Jamaica, January 1957.

Washington, D.C., June 1957.

RIGHT:
Charleston, South Carolina, November 1962.

Nuns clamming on Long Island,
September 1957.

Portuguese girl, April 1946.
This photograph was taken for the Portuguese Tourist Bureau.

Above and right: Charleston, South Carolina, November 1962.

Mrs. Stanford White and her great-granddaughter Suzannah Lessard.
Harper's Bazaar, January 1949.

People

Mr. and Mrs. Harold Vanderbilt at tea in Lantana, Florida,
with his sister Mme. Jacques Balsan and her granddaughter
and great-grandson, January 1950.

*"My favorite subject is people. Catching them unawares, at the one precise
moment that never returns, is to me the greatest thrill of all. To register on
film their joy, suffering, anger, or happiness brings me the deepest
satisfaction."*

Dinner at "Heron Bay," the home of Ronald and Marietta Tree,
Barbados, February 1961.

*"Ronnie and Marietta Tree's house is the most beautiful tropical dream
house I have seen anywhere. It is a Paladian-columned coral gem."*

Mrs. Charleton Henry, Philadelphia, October 1950.
Harper's Bazaar.

Mrs. Walter B. Allan, Mill Reef Club, Antigua, British West Indies.
Sports Illustrated, 1959.

"I stayed with a wonderful woman called Mrs. Allan, who wore becoming flowered dresses and straw hats that suited her size and made her look chic. She had a charming pink house with an open dining room, where yellow banana quits and emerald hummingbirds flew back and forth at breakfast."

Konrad Adenauer, October 1961.

"I was told that he was cold as ice and that I would not like him. When I went into his office, I said, 'This is a great honor, Mr. Adenauer.' He said, 'Sit down, sit down. I have plenty of time. Everyone is always telling me to hurry. This is a great mistake.' I spent the next hour taking portraits of him. He had a marvelous skull-like head, and he seemed much younger than his years."

Gloria Vanderbilt at her home in Connecticut.
Vogue, February 1966.

LEFT:
Lauri Peters, actress, in the stage production of
The Sound of Music, July 1960.

Mike Todd at the Jones Beach Theater on Long Island, 1952.

"I renewed my acquaintance with Mike Todd when we went to see a beautiful production of A Night in Venice *at Jones Beach. The stage was built on a revolving island, and the audience was in an arena on the other side of the water. The show had everything, from real floating gondolas to bursting fireworks. When I realized that the producer of the spectacle was Mike Todd, I went to the box office and left my name. Mike arrived with the speed of lightning. Before the evening was over, we mutually agreed that I would return the next day to photograph him on the set. One couldn't take a bad picture of Mike. Of course I photographed him in a gondola."*

RIGHT:
Senator John F. Kennedy and Jacqueline Bouvier on their wedding day,
Newport, Rhode Island, September 1953.

"The Kennedy family was somewhat overwhelming. There are so many of them and they are so vital that they are bound to take over any place like a swarm of locusts. At a quarter to one, a big limousine drove into the portico. It was a radiant Jackie and her handsome newlywed husband. When she saw me with my camera, she said, 'Toni is a good friend of mine. Let's give her a chance to get a good picture before the guests arrive.' "

Mary Martin during the run of *South Pacific* on Broadway.
McCall's, 1949.

RIGHT:
Lilli Palmer and her husband, Rex Harrison, 1950.

Gloria Guinness, her daughter Dolores Guinness,
and her grandson Loel Guinness, Palm Beach, April 1962.

Kirk Douglas, Klosters, Switzerland, 1954.

William Styron.
Vogue, May 1968.

Mrs. John Pringle and Michael Duplaix at the
William S. Paley cottage, Round Hill, Jamaica.
Sports Illustrated, February 1957.

Mrs. Lucy Lynn in formal fox-hunting sidesaddle attire
at Foxcroft School, Thanksgiving Day, 1953.

LEFT:
Miss Charlotte Haxall Noland, founder of Foxcroft School, in sidesaddle
habit, Middleburg, Virginia, 1949.
From the exhibit "Man in Sports."

*"My first meeting with Miss Charlotte was at the age of fourteen. Mother thought the time had arrived to
look around for a finishing school, so over Thanksgiving we went to be looked over at Foxcroft, in the
heart of fox-hunting country in Virginia. We arrived at the school to meet a cavalcade of girls in full hunt
regalia. At the head was a magnificent white-haired, top-hatted, and veiled woman turned out in blue
riding habit. She was riding sidesaddle. As she rode out of the school, she turned to her girls and sang out,
'Ride like hell, little darlings! Ride like hell!' I was enchanted. Years later, after I started photographing, I
went to photograph Miss Charlotte. We became tremendous friends, and I often stayed at 'Covert,' her
house. She once said, 'I consider you one of my girls. Why didn't you come to Foxcroft?' I answered, 'I
tried, but you wouldn't have me, Miss Charlotte.' "*

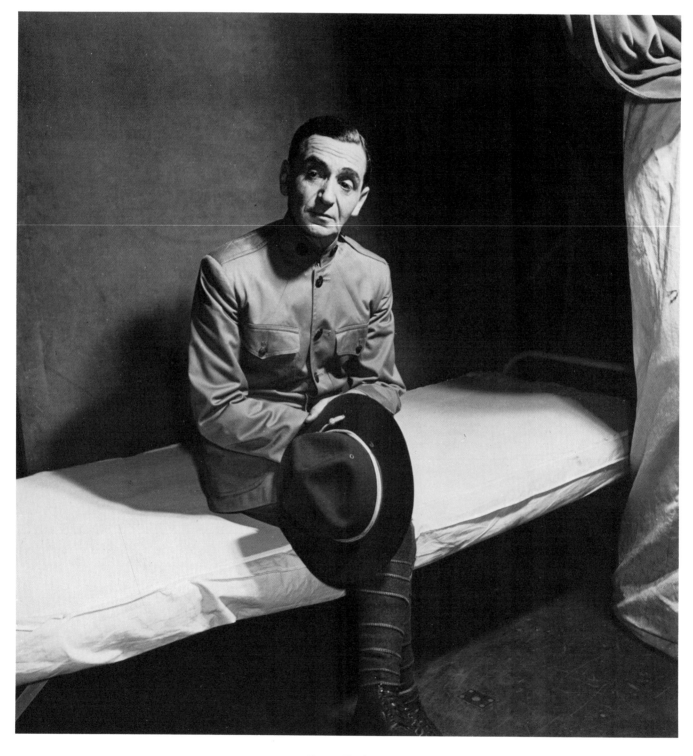

Irving Berlin.
Vogue, July 1942.

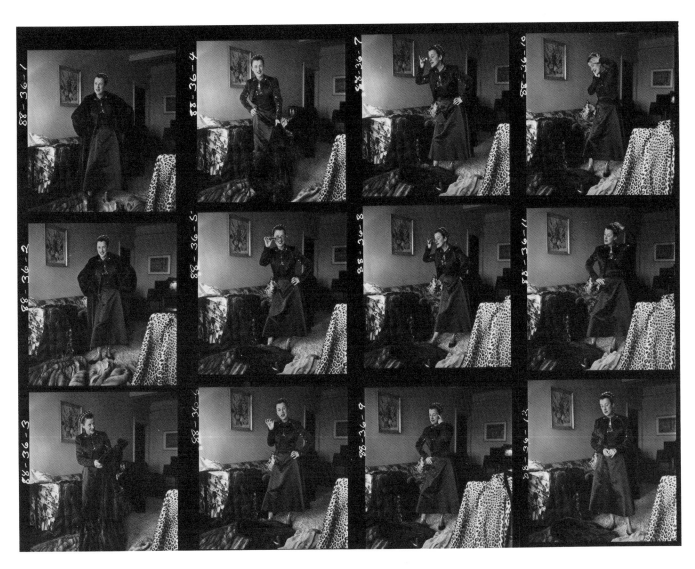

Beatrice Lillie.
Town and Country, August 1948.

Mme. Jacques Balsan, the former Consuelo Vanderbilt,
Duchess of Marlborough, at home near Palm Beach, May 1950.

The Duke of Windsor, golfing, May 1953.

Toni Frissell with dog Hugo at Stony Brook Harbor.
Photograph by Sidney Frissell Stafford. *Vogue*, June 1973.

"Now I'm sixty-six and I love it."

Acknowledgments

I would like to express my gratitude to all who have helped me over the past five years in making this book possible:

Beverly Brannan, Curator of Photography, Library of Congress, without whose gentle push and never-ending advice and help there would never have been a book; Carol Johnson, Assistant Curator of Photography, Library of Congress, and Arlene Hughes and Pete Richey, Library of Congress Technicians, who located the appropriate negatives from the nearly 275,000 options; Martin Rhatigan, my friend, whose enthusiasm and belief in my mother's work offered me encouragement and helped shape the book from the beginning; Connie Fisher, fellow photographer and friend, who was so helpful in making the first choices for presentation from more than 25,000 enlargements from my mother's collection; Thomas Watson, Jr., a friend of my mother's, who gave me the guidance and drive to get me started; Cooby Greenway, my cousin, who lived in Washington and did research for me when I couldn't make it there myself; Diana Edkins, Curator of Photographs and Manager of Rights and Permissions, Condé Nast Publications, for her ideas, generosity, and support; George Plimpton, editor of *The Paris Review* and author, and a friend of my mother's, whose Introduction perfectly captures her multifaceted personality. And from Doubleday: Jacqueline Kennedy Onassis, Senior Editor, for whose efforts no written or spoken words would ever be adequate to express my thanks; Bruce Tracy, Editor, for his organizational wizardry and positive attitude; Nancy Tuckerman, Senior Publicist, to whom I will always be indebted for so much; Marysarah Quinn, Design Director, whose contributions are evident on every page of this book; Peter Kruzan, Art Director, for his unparalleled eye for finding and creating the best; and Scott Moyers, Assistant Editor, Mr. Details, for his bubbling enthusiasm and forever smile.

Sidney Frissell Stafford

Photograph
Negative Numbers

The following list provides the negative numbers for photographs reproduced from the Toni Frissell Collection in the Library of Congress. Prints of Frissell photographs may be ordered from the Library's Photoduplication Service, Washington, D.C. 20540-5230. The first two positions (positions are separated by hyphens) indicate the Library of Congress and the Frissell Collection. For those interested in determining the size of the original negatives, 01 and 02 after the F9 in the numbers below indicate 2¼ x 2¼ inches, and 03 and 04 indicate 35mm. Other codes indicate various sizes of copy negatives, generally made by Miss Frissell. The year and month that a photograph was made appear in the fourth position of the negative numbers. The final two positions refer to film rolls and frames.

Commercial use of photographs produced for hire by Toni Frissell may be restricted through copyright. It is the responsibility of the researcher to investigate issues of copyright. An information sheet about the Frissell Collection is available from the Prints and Photographs Division.

PAGE NUMBER	NEGATIVE NUMBER	PAGE NUMBER	NEGATIVE NUMBER
49	LC-F9-04-6102-025-33	101	LC-F9-02-5407-032-09
50	LC-F9-04-6306-014-22	102	From private collection
51	LC-F9-04-5903-008-36	103	LC-F9-04-6712-017-29. By permission of King Ranch, Inc.
52	LC-F9-02-5005-029-05		
53	LC-F9-04-6204-014-10	104 top	LC-F9-04-5708-008-27
54	LC-F9-04-6206-021-32A	104 bottom	LC-F9-04-5912-001-32
55	LC-F9-52-5709-52A-26	105	LC-F9-01-4703-044-06
56	LC-F9-02-4101-41-12	106	LC-F9-03-5312-063-17
57	LC-F9-04-6305-012-08	107	LC-F9-02-4911-031-03
58	LC-F9-02-4912-025-01	108	LC-F9-04-6308-024-09
59	LC-F9-04-6403-002-34	109	LC-F9-02-5310-123-11
60	No negative at Library of Congress	110	LC-F9-04-5611-070-05
61	LC-F9-04-5806-05-19A	111	LC-F9-03-5311-031-21
62	LC-F9-03-3907-066-05	112	LC-F9-01-5205-011-04
63	LC-F9-02-4605-602-08	113	LC-F9-01-4910-036-11
64	LC-F9-02-4605-052-10	114	LC-F9-04-6011-012-08
65	LC-F9-04-6009-042-21	115	LC-F9-02-4304-056-11
66	LC-F9-04-5705-025-08	116	LC-F9-04-6212-007-08
67	LC-F9-02-4704-092-06	117	LC-F9-04-6211-155-30
68	LC-F9-01-4406-043-06	118–119	From private collection
69	LC-F9-01-4009-037-11	120	LC-F9-02-4810-173-09
70	LC-F9-04-6306-005-22	121	LC-F9-02-5701-038-05
71	LC-F9-02-5708-043-08	122	LC-F9-02-5706-053-07
72 top	LC-F9-04-5705-027-04	123	LC-F9-04-6211-163-22
72 bottom	LC-F9-04-6112-004-16	124	LC-F9-04-5709-011-06
73	LC-F9-49-6009-041-03	125	LC-F9-01-4605-629-08
74	LC-F9-04-6105-006-05	126	LC-F9-49-6211-164-24
75	LC-F9-06-6306-002-29	127	LC-F9-04-6211-167-27
76	No negative at Library of Congress	128	No negative at Library of Congress
77	LC-F9-49-5306-026-02	129	LC-F9-04-5901-013-18
78	LC-F9-04-6304-014-12	130	LC-F9-04-6102-019-05
79	LC-F9-03-5007-107-19	131	LC-F9-02-5008-017-11
80	LC-F9-02-5306-071-04	132	LC-F9-04-5901-022-25
81	LC-F9-02-5306-072-10	133	LC-F9-02-6110-013
82	LC-F9-02-5007-041-09	134	LC-F9-04-6007-031-38
83	LC-F9-04-5306-002-30	135	LC-F9-04-6506-040-21
84	From private collection	136	LC-F9-02-5208-074-06
85	LC-F9-03-5306-003-33	137	LC-F9-04-5309-013-28
86	LC-F9-03-5306-107-06	138	LC-F9-01-4908-015-11
87	LC-F9-02-5007-024-10	139	LC-F9-01-5010-004-06
88	LC-F9-04-6304-009-05	140	LC-F9-04-6204-011-34
89	LC-F9-02-5006-059-01	141	LC-F9-04-5401-042-12
90	LC-F9-50-5006-from color. No original negative at Library of Congress	142	LC-F9-04-6709-017-37
		143	From private collection
91	LC-F9-02-5007-061-12	144	LC-F9-01-4911-032-10
92	LC-F9-02-4308-071-07. By permission of King Ranch, Inc.	145	LC-F9-04-5312-004-20
		146	LC-F9-02-4207-037-06
94–95	LC-F9-49-5310-102-08	147	LC-F9-01-4808-36-01 through -12
96	LC-F9-02-5611-082-01	148	From color, no original negative at Library of Congress
97	LC-F9-02-5310-094-04		
98	LC-F9-04-5611-035-04	149	LC-F9-03-5305-044-29
99	LC-F9-02-4411-016-03		
100	LC-F9-02-4309-044-02. By permission of King Ranch, Inc.